AMAZING SPORTS

TENNIS

BY LORI DITTMER

CREATIVE EDUCATION • CREATIVE PAPERBACKS

Published by Creative Education and Creative Paperbacks
P.O. Box 227, Mankato, Minnesota 56002
Creative Education and Creative Paperbacks are imprints of
The Creative Company
www.thecreativecompany.us

Design by The Design Lab
Production by Dana Koehler
Art direction by Rita Marshall
Printed in the United States of America

Photographs by Alamy (North Wind Picture Archives, Vit Simanek/CTK Photo/Alamy Live News), Dreamstime (Zhukovsky), iStockphoto (amriphoto, razihusin), Shutterstock (art3, Olga Besnard, Neale Cousland, Everett Collection, Mai Groves, Rena Schild, Supermop, Yurii Vydyborets, Leonard Zhukovsky)

Copyright © 2020 Creative Education, Creative Paperbacks
International copyright reserved in all countries. No part of this book may be reproduced in any form without written permission from the publisher.

Library of Congress Cataloging-in-Publication Data
Names: Dittmer, Lori, author.
Title: Tennis / Lori Dittmer.
Series: Amazing sports.
Includes index.
Summary: Get the ball rolling with this high-interest introduction to tennis, the sport known for its low nets and rackets. Also included is a biographical story about professional tennis players Venus and Serena Williams.

Identifiers:
ISBN 978-1-64026-215-7 (hardcover)
ISBN 978-1-62832-778-6 (pbk)
ISBN 978-1-64000-350-7 (eBook)
This title has been submitted for CIP processing under LCCN 2019937882.

First Edition HC 9 8 7 6 5 4 3 2 1
First Edition PBK 9 8 7 6 5 4 3 2 1

Table of Contents

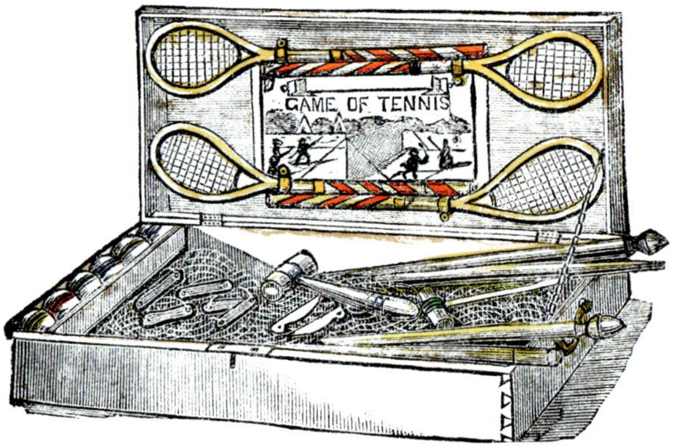

Hundreds of years ago, people in France played a "game of the palm." They used their hands to hit a ball instead of a racket. In the 1870s, Major Walter Wingfield made a book of rules. His game became known as lawn tennis.

Lawn tennis sets of the late 1800s included all the pieces needed to play.

Each player uses a racket. A lightweight racket with a large head is good for beginners. Players hit a tennis ball over a net. The net stands three feet (0.9 m) high in the middle of the court.

Naomi Osaka started playing tennis as a child, coached by her dad.

Hitting the ball back over the net after a serve is called a return.

People play tennis outside or inside. The surface can be grass, clay, or **hard court**. Singles play on a smaller court. Doubles play on a wider surface. Players take turns serving the ball from behind the baseline.

hard court a tennis court with a hard surface such as asphalt or concrete

FILA

Tennis can be a one-on-one game. This is called singles tennis. For doubles, two pairs face off. A competition is called a match.

In 2006, James Blake was number four in the world for singles players.

A match is broken down into games and sets. To win the game, a player or pair must be the first to score four points. The first to win six games wins the set. Players who take the most sets win the match.

Tennis scores from zero to three points are called "love," "15," "30," and "40."

MELBOURNE
KIA
KIA
KIA
ROLEX
2:10

UNI
QLO

During a match, players must return the ball without letting it bounce more than once. In doubles, the pair decides which areas of the court they will play.

Novak Djokovic has a two-handed backhand and is one of the world's best.

Doubles players divide their side in half. One person plays closer to the net. Officials watch to see if the ball lands out of bounds.

The player closest to the net plays at the service line.

Rio2016

A team from the Czech Republic beat the Williams sisters at the 2016 Olympics.

The Association of Tennis Professionals (ATP) and the Women's Tennis Association (WTA) are groups for pro tennis players. Pros play in major tournaments like Wimbledon, the US Open, the Australian Open, and the French Open. Tennis has been a part of the Summer **Olympic Games** since 1988.

Olympic Games a set of international sports competitions which take place every four years

WTA star Caroline Wozniacki has won 30 singles titles.

Tennis is fun for all ages and skill levels. Grab a friend and a racket. Practice keeping score. Or just try to get a **rally** going! There are many ways to enjoy this amazing game.

rally a sequence of back-and-forth shots between players

Story of Players: Venus and Serena Williams

Sisters Venus and Serena Williams grew up playing tennis in Los Angeles. Their father, Richard, wanted them to go pro. He helped them practice every day. The girls went professional as teenagers. Since then, they have become some of the most famous tennis stars in the world. They have faced off against each other 30 times in major tournaments. But they also play together. They have won three gold medals in women's doubles in the Summer Olympics.

Read More

Gifford, Clive. *Sports Skills: Tennis*. London: Franklin Watts, 2017.

Rausch, David. *United States Tennis Association*. Minneapolis: Bellwether Media, 2015.

Websites

DK Find Out: Tennis
https://www.dkfindout.com/us/sports/tennis/
Read about the parts of a tennis racket.

Ducksters: Sports – Tennis
https://www.ducksters.com/sports/tennis.php
Learn more about tennis courts and how to play the game.

Note: Every effort has been made to ensure that the websites listed above are suitable for children, that they have educational value, and that they contain no inappropriate material. However, because of the nature of the Internet, it is impossible to guarantee that these sites will remain active indefinitely or that their contents will not be altered.

Index